Covi

The Kõpu Lighthouse on the Estonian island of Hiiumaa has been a well-known tourist attraction since 1999. It is one of the oldest lighthouses globally, and since its completion in 1531, it has been in continuous use. Several reconstructions were made to the structure by the Swedish and Russian Empires between the 17th and 21st centuries. The Kõpu Lighthouse lost its role as a primary navigation aid in 1997 when a radar lighthouse was built. However, due to its popularity and memorable shape, it is often used as a symbol of Hiiumaa.

Photo Attribution: By Inmedialv @ https://depositphotos.com/11850 2628/stock-photo-kopu-lighthouse-in-saaremaa-estonia.html

COUNTRY JUMPER in Estonia

Copyright © 2020

All rights reserved. No part of this book may be used or reproduced in any manner whatsoever without written permission, except in the case of reprints in the context of review.

Contact Author at:
countryjumperbooks@gmail.com

Website:
countryjumperbooks.net

Hello boys and girls! Do you know how many countries are in the world today? The answer will depend a lot on how a "country" is defined. Some countries are members of the United Nations, others are not, and some are given only partial recognition. However, they are just as important to learn about. Which country do you live in?

My name is COUNTRY JUMPER, and I'd like you to come and jump with me around the world. I've selected 205 countries to visit, so put on your Jumping Shoes and buckle up. Today we are visiting Estonia, a country in the continent of Europe.

Table of Contents

Chapter 1: Facts

Chapter 2: Terrain and Climate

Chapter 3: Politics

Chapter 4: Education

Chapter 5: Transportation

Chapter 6: Holidays and Festivals

Chapter 7: Animal, Bird, and Flower

Chapter 8: Popular Foods

Chapter 9: Money

Chapter 10: Sports

Chapter 11: Music and Instruments

Chapter 12: Clothing

Chapter 13: Fun Places for Kids to Visit

Chapter 14: Other Interesting Facts

Facts About Estonia

The Estonians are believed to have originated from the Finno-Ugric tribes. The name Estonia was used for the first time to describe the region in 100 CE. Estonia's first invaders were the Vikings, who were passing through the area during the mid-9th century. In the 11th and 12th centuries, the Russians made numerous incursions into Estonians but failed to establish control. However, in the 13th century, Estonia came under the rulership of the Livonian Brothers of the Sword, a German religious order and their Danish allies, who occupied northern Estonia. The Livonian Brothers of the Sword later merged with the Teutonic Order and became known as the Livonian Order. Estonia was split in two, and the Teutonic Order ruled southern Estonia while the Danes ruled the north. The King of Denmark later sold northern Estonia for 19,000 Cologne marks to the Teutonic Order in 1346. German rule under the Teutonic Order was followed by Swedish control, beginning in northern Estonia in 1561. The Livonian

War from 1558 and 1582, between Russia (led by Ivan the Terrible), Poland, Denmark, and Sweden, resulted in the Swedes controlling northern and western Estonia, Poland controlling the south, and Denmark ruling over the island of Saaremaa. The Polish-Swedish War that began in 1600 was a long war for control of Estonia and Livonia. It lasted until 1629, and Sweden gained control of Livonia, southern Estonia, northern Latvia, and Saaremaa. Between 1695 and 1697, Estonia experienced The Great Famine that killed off almost 20 percent of Estonian's population. The Great Northern War, occurring between 1700 and 1721, was a conflict between Russia (led by Peter the Great) and its allies and Sweden. The war resulted in the decline of Swedish influence and Russia's emergence as a major power in that region, which led to Estonia being controlled by Russia. In 1917, a revolution broke out, and when the German army marched into Estonia, the Russian Communists fled. Estonia proclaimed its first independence in February 1918, which lasted for only two decades. Nazi Germany and the USSR negotiated a secret pact in 1939, essentially handing Estonia over to the Soviet Union. In 1990, Estonia declared the restoration of its independence from the Soviet Union, and the country's pre-1940 state of independence was eventually restored on August 20, 1991. The capital of Estonia is Tallinn. The country's population in late 2020 was around 1,326,800.

Estonia's national flag was first adopted on November 21, 1918, after the country declared its independence. The flag has a tricolor design featuring three equal horizontal bands of blue at the top, black in the center, and white at the bottom. The interpretation of the colors has blue, representing the **sky and the Baltic sea. The black color symbolizing past oppression, fertile soil, and the black greatcoat of an Estonian man.** The white color depicts Estonia's aspiration towards light and **purity and pursuit of a brighter future.** The flag was outlawed in 1940; however, with the loosening of Soviet control in 1988, it was reinstated.

Estonia's coat of arms was adopted on June 19, 1925, and again on October 16, 1990. The country uses two versions. The official emblem has a golden shield featuring a picture of three blue lions with red tongues. Golden oak branches are on both sides of the shield. The insignia is derived from Denmark's coat of arms, which ruled northern Estonia in the thirteenth century. The three lions are derived from the arms of Danish king Valdemar II who conquered northern Estonia in 1219.

A country's national coat of arms is a symbol that signifies an independent state in the form of a heraldic achievement. An important use for national coats of arms is as the main symbol on the cover of passports.

Estonian is the official language of the country. It belongs to the Finnic branch of the Uralic languages. Estonian is closely related to Finnish, which is spoken in Finland, across the other side of the Gulf of Finland. It is one of the few languages of Europe that is not of an Indo-European origin. Although the Estonian and Germanic languages are of very different origins, many similar words are easily identifiable in Estonian and German. Russian is the second most spoken language in the country. Other languages include Belarussian, Finnish, Latvian, and Ukrainian.

Christianity was introduced to Estonia in the 11th century, and the country is historically a Lutheran Protestant nation. Only around 14 percent of the population has declared religion an important part of their daily life. Therefore, Estonia is considered one of the least religious countries in the world regarding its attitude toward religion. Other religions include Eastern Orthodox, Baptists, Islam, Jehovah's Witnesses, Methodists, Mormon, and Roman Catholics. There are also smaller congregations that have not applied for official registration in Estonia.

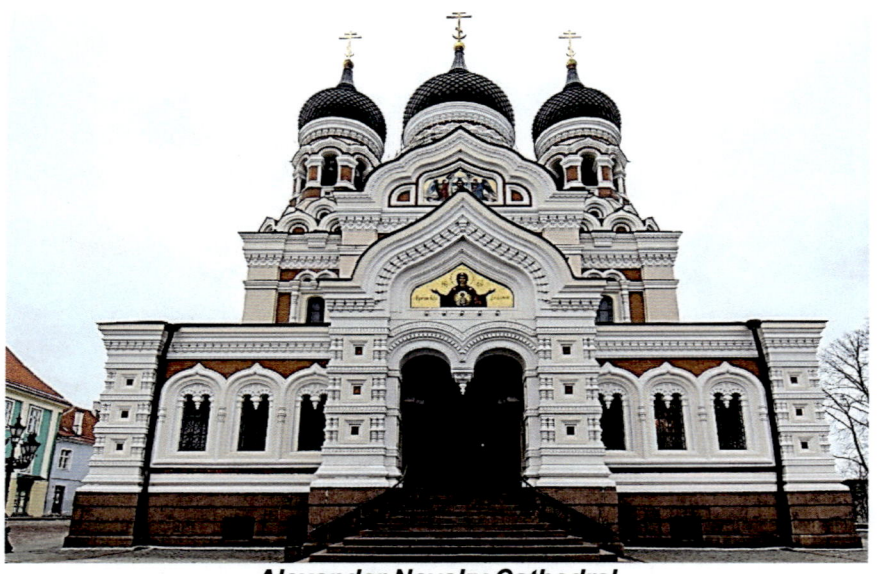

Alexander Nevsky Cathedral
Image by Jaafar Alnasser @ https://www.flickr.com/photos/jaafaralnasser/12962313753

Terrain and Climate of Estonia

Estonia's terrain consists of green land, and around half of the country is covered with forests. It is a flat country with a shallow coastline along the Baltic Sea. The country's highest point is Suur Munamägi, also known as Egg Mountain. This mountain reaches 1,043 feet above sea level. Estonia's climate is temperate and mild, with warm summers and severe winters. The weather is frequently breezy and humid due to the close proximity of the Baltic Sea, and the seasons vary widely.

Photo 189205251 © anda mikelsone | Dreamstime.com

Politics of Estonia

The political system of Estonia takes place in the framework of a parliamentary republic. The prime minister heads the current government. The president is the chief of the state, and is elected for a five-year term, which is renewable once. This individual is nominated by the prime minister and approved by the parliament. The legislature in Estonia is unicameral, which means that it is a government with one legislative body. Estonia has a transparent system where government decisions are almost instantly made public.

Seat of the Parliament of Estonia in Toompea Castle
Image by Kaupo Kalda @ https://commons.wikimedia.org/w/index.php?curid=57932969

Education in Estonia

Education is compulsory for grades one through nine in Estonia. The educational system is divided into four levels as follows: 1) preschool, 2) primary (grades one to six), 3) lower secondary (grades seven to nine), and 4) upper secondary (grades 10 to 12). Estonia has one of the best educational systems in Europe because of its innovative education model. There are currently around twenty universities in Estonia. The largest and oldest one is the University of Tartu, which was founded in 1632.

University of Tartu
Image by Ivar Leidus @ https://commons.wikimedia.org/w/index.php?curid=21406217

Transportation in Estonia

Transportation in Estonia consists of bus, tram, trolleybus, train, and ferry service. Estonia is the first country to offer free public transit nationwide. The free ride is based on certain conditions, and riders must register for the service. Trams and trolleybuses are only available in the city of Tallinn. The first tram route was opened in 1888. The rail network in Estonia is very reliable, and it is fast and comfortable. Each municipal area has its own bus service. The Lennart Meri Tallinn Airport is the main airport in Estonia. It is considered one of the best airports in Europe.

Tram
Image by Pjotr Mahhonin @ https://commons.wikimedia.org/w/index.php?curid=70857094

Holidays and Festivals in Estonia

On August 20, 1991, Estonia declared independence during the Soviet military coup attempt in Moscow, restoring the pre-1940 state. Since then, August 20 has been acknowledged as the day of the Restoration of Independence for Estonians. The holiday was first celebrated in 1992 following the disbanding of the Soviet Union. The day is celebrated with many flying flags, the closure of most businesses, and a sense of jubilation.

The Tallinn Old Town Days Festival is a week-long festival that occurs in late May or early June. This event was first organized in 1982 and is one of the city's biggest annual events. Each year, the festival follows a different slogan, which inspires the theme of the festival. Some featured themes are Children's Day, Music Day, and Medieval Day. The day is celebrated with dancing, concerts, storytelling, historical tours, and costumed performers. People attending the event are dressed in ancient clothing, such as knights in armor, to create an ancient setting. Visitors who want to take part in that tradition can purchase ancient costumes from local markets.

Animal, Bird, Plant of Estonia

The grey wolf was selected as Estonia's national animal in 2018. This wolf is the most popular animal in Estonian folk traditions; and symbolizes wild and untouched nature. The grey wolf is tough, sturdy, and extremely smart. It is distinguished from coyotes and jackals based on its broader snout, shorter ears, shorter torso, and a longer tail. The wolf can reduce blood flow near the skin in cold climates to conserve its body heat. They are found in habitats such as deserts, plains, forests, and tundra.

Image by Wolf Kolmården @ https://commons.wikimedia.org/w/index.php?curid=12423176

The barn swallow is the national bird of Estonia. The barn swallow's selection as its national bird was mainly the result of a campaign conducted at the beginning of the sixties. The barn swallow has a steely blue back, tail and wings, and reddish-brown to tawny underparts. Male feathers are more colorful than the female's. Its call can be heard from virtually every eave or barn rafter in the country. The bird is found in habitats such as coastal waters, fields, meadows, parks, and ponds. Barn swallows sometimes join different swallow species in mixed hunting flocks.

Image by I. Malene @ https://commons.wikimedia.org/w/index.php?curid=20612

The cornflower was chosen as a national symbol in Estonia in 1968. However, it has been a folk emblem for many years before that time. The cornflower is the symbol of the People's Union political party. The upper stripe on the Estonian flag is frequently referred to as cornflower blue. Young Estonian girls wear the blue cornflower as part of the traditional garlands for festivals, and it is also often used as an artistic motif in local folk art. Cornflowers are considered endangered due to the over-use of herbicides.

Image by Kiran Jonnalagadda @ https://commons.wikimedia.org/w/index.php?curid=9420942

Popular Foods of Estonia

Mulgipuder is a national dish of Estonia. It is a rustic porridge consisting of mashed cereal grains and potatoes. Bacon and sautéed onions are sometimes added for extra flavor. This dish can be served as the main course, as a side dish, and also with sour cream and rye bread. Mulgipuder is often associated with Southern Estonia; however, this comfort food is enjoyed throughout the country as a home-cooked meal and served in restaurants.

A popular soup in Estonia is called leivasupp, a unique black, sweet bread soup that is often made with mashed bread, raisins, fruit juice, cinnamon, and sugar. It is typically prepared with rye bread and is usually accompanied by milk, sour cream, whipped cream, fresh fruit, and nuts. When preparing this soup, the bread loaves are cooked gently while stirring in water. The bread is put through a sieve and placed in the liquid with the other ingredients. Leivasupp is a popular school lunch in Estonia that can be served warm or chilled. It is also enjoyed as a dessert or a light afternoon snack.

Image by Anton Klink @ https://www.flickr.com/photos/95393545@N03/17399878062

Kohuke is a curd snack prepared with pressed curd cheese and additional ingredients such as sugar, sweetener, or other products. This sweet snack can be prepared with added fillings such as raisins or jams and comes in various flavors such as vanilla, chocolate, or caramel. It is often covered in a chocolate coating and can also be decorated with fruits, coconut flakes, poppy seeds, or chocolate bits. This is a cold refrigerated snack that can be prepared at home or purchased in stores throughout the Baltic region.

Image by Bearas @ https://commons.wikimedia.org/w/index.php?curid=15086875

Money in Estonia

The official currency of Estonia is the euro (Code: EUR). One euro is a base unit, made up of 100 cents. The euro is the second most traded currency on the foreign exchange market and is used by 19 European countries that make up the eurozone. Estonia was the first former Soviet Union Republic to adopt the euro in 2011 as its currency. The previous currency was the Estonian kroon, which was used for two periods in Estonia's history from 1928–1940 and 1992–2011. The word kroon is related to the Nordic currencies and is derived from the Latin word corona.

Sports in Estonia

Sports is a vital part of the Estonian culture, and Estonia was one of the countries that participated during the early parts of the Olympics. Basketball is one of the country's most popular sports. Other sports include beach volleyball, cricket, cycling, judo, and football (soccer). Estonia has also produced several world-class cyclists. Kiiking is a sport that was invented in Estonia. The objective of the game is to pass over the spindle with the swing. Swinging on a kiiking swing is usually done in an upright position and by using a specific squatting technique.

Kiiking
Image by Eesti Kiikingi Liit @ https://commons.wikimedia.org/wiki/File:Kiiking_15.JPG

Music and Instruments of Estonia

The history of music in Estonia dates back to the 12th century. The older folksongs, referred to as runic songs, were gradually replaced by rhythmic folksongs in the 18th century. Rustic, pop, rock, classical, and alternative are some of Estonia's other music genres. Musical instruments include the accordion, bagpipes, concertina, fiddle, and zither. The kannel is a native instrument, and it is the oldest known instrument in the country, believed to have been around for about two thousand years.

Kannel
Image by Jassu Hertsmann @ https://commons.wikimedia.org/w/index.php?curid=31867324

Traditional Clothing in Estonia

Information on traditional clothing worn in Estonia dates back to the 11th through the 13th centuries. National outfits were indicators of status and national origin. Historical national clothes such as linen shirts, woolen skirts, trousers, embroidered accessories, knit socks, and beads resemble those of many European regions. Garments worn by ancient women consisted of a linen chemise with long sleeves and a woolen coat. A woolen piece of cloth was wrapped around the hips, and it was accompanied by a belt.

Fun Places for Kids to Visit in Estonia

Atlantis H2O Aquapark is a waterpark and nature center in Estonia. Visitors get to meet the water bear and blue whale and leave the park with a better understanding of water science. There are several water attractions, such as a wave pool, circulating pool, and eight different slides. The longest slide is more than a hundred meters. The slides are color-coded and offer different experiences. For example, the purple slide is only for experienced swimmers, and the black and yellow slides have light effects, and single and double tubes are allowed.

The Skywheel of Tallinn is a unique attraction in Estonia that provides an amazing view of the city and the Baltic Sea. The observation Ferris wheel reaches a height of 120 meters above sea level. It has 27 weatherproof gondolas that provide safe and comfortable rides year-round. The gondolas have air conditioning for rides during the summer, and each of them can accommodate up to six people who can stand or sit while inside the gondola. The Skywheel in Estonia offers the same view as the largest Ferris wheels in the world. The Skywheel is available to schools and youth groups to conduct classes or host graduation.

Visitors can tour hidden tunnels underneath Old Town Tallinn. The Swedes originally built the tunnels for defense in the 17th and 18th centuries. The tunnels served as walls for ammunition, troop movement, and to spy on the enemy. They were eventually renovated into bomb shelters during World War II. The tunnels later became a refuge for punk rockers and a sanctuary for the homeless. Many people sought refuge in the tunnels to escape from the harsh winters until the authorities kicked them out in the mid-2000s. The tunnels later became a tourist attraction. Some areas still have that medieval look and feel.

Other Interesting Facts About Estonia

- The country was once ruled by the Danish, the Swedish, the Germans, and the Russians.
- In area, Estonia is about twice the size of New Jersey.
- Lake Peipsi is Estonia's largest lake and Europe's fourth-largest freshwater lake.
- Estonians celebrate their independence twice a year. Once on the 24th of February and the other on the 20th of August.
- The Skype software was developed in Estonia.
- Estonia is the birthplace of the first Christmas tree.
- It is a law in Estonia to have safety reflectors attached when walking or biking at night time.
- Estonia is among the cleanest places on the planet earth to breathe.
- Estonians are very beautiful and have the highest number of supermodels per capita in the world.
- Estonian population is declining.
- Estonia has been described as one of the most internet-focused countries in Europe.
- It has one of the highest rates of mobile phone ownership per capita.
- The country is among the top three bird-watching destinations in Europe.

Eswatini, a country in Southern Africa, is the next stop on our journey. The air travel distance between Estonia and ***Eswatini*** is approximately 5,873 miles. It takes around 10.49 hours to travel between the two countries.

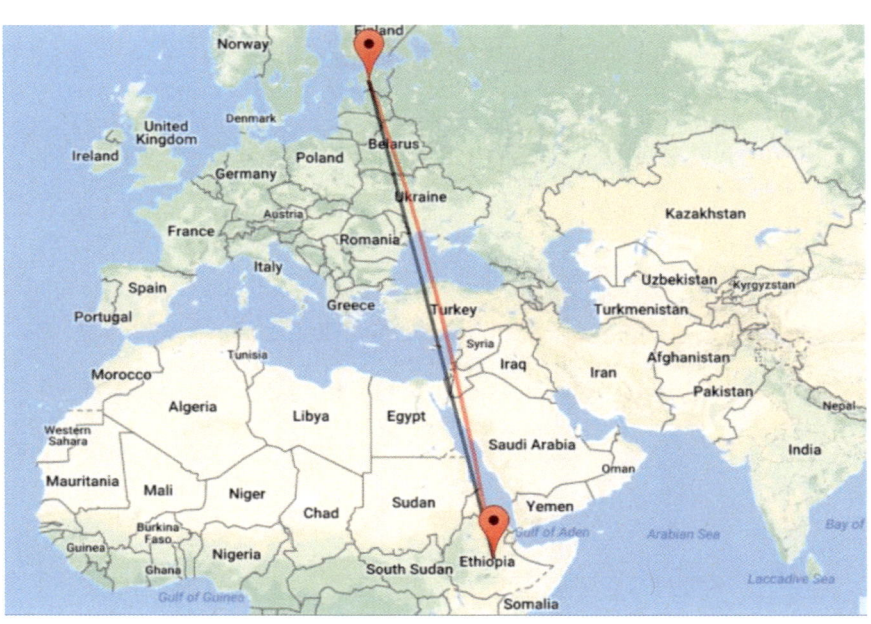

REFERENCES

1. https://www.spottinghistory.com/view/455/kopu-lighthouse/
2. https://www.globalroadwarrior.com/estonia/historical-timeline.html
3. https://en.wikipedia.org/wiki/Estonia
4. http://www.worldometers.info/world-population/estonia-population/
5. https://wikitravel.org/en/Estonian_phrasebook
6. www.studyinestonia.ee/nature-and-climate
7. hhttps://www.nordetrade.com/en/explore-new-market/Estonia/political-context
8. https://education.stateunivetrsity.com/pages/44/estonia-educational-system-overview.html
9. https://www.lonelyplanet.com/estonia/tallinn/events/old-town-days/a/poi-fes/1275698/359139
10. http://estonianworld.com/life/estonia-celebrates-the-day-of-restoration-of-independence/
11. https://europea.org/estonia-has-a-national-animal
12. https://en.wikipedia.org/wiki/Wolf
13. https://www.allaboutbirds.org/guide/Barn_Swallow
14. https://www.globalroadwarrior.com/estonia/national-flower.html
15. https://www.tasteatlas.com/mulgipuder
16. https://worldfood.guide/dish/leivasupp/
17. https://www.tasteatlas.com/kohuke
18. https://www.smoney.com.au/blog/currency-in-estonia/
19. https://en.wikipedia.org/wiki/Estonian_kroon
20. http://www.topendsports.com/world/countries/estonia.htm
21. https://www.visitestonia.com/en/why-estonia/kiiking-a-wild-sport-invented-in-estonia
22. https://en.wikipedia.org/wiki/Music_of_Estonia
23. http://eestikultuurist.ut.ee/rahvariided/index.php/en/estonian-folk-costumes
24. https://aquapark.ee/liutorud/
25. https://superskypark.ee/toode/vaateratas/
26. https://www.argophilia.com/news/bastion-tunnels-tallinn/28415/
27. http://thefactfile.org/interesting-facts-estonia/3/
28. https://www.distancefromto.net/distance-from-estonia-to-ethiopia

Continue following COUNTRY JUMPER as he treks across the globe from countries A through Z. Why stop here when there is so much more to learn about this great big world? Where will the next jump take you? You can follow COUNTRY JUMPER on his journey from A through Z or jump into the countries that you are curious to learn more about. A total of 205 books representing each country will be available in this series. If you cannot find a country that you would like to explore, please contact the author.

Happy reading!

Made in the USA
Columbia, SC
27 April 2023